Graphic Design

The Ultimate Beginners Guide To Mastering The Art Of Graphic Design

By *Jennifer Inston*

Introduction

The years of digital art has been around since technology and the internet became active in our global society. "Graphic designing is relatively a new field that emerged as an independent subject in the mid-twentieth century. Its development dates back to late 19th century when the first printed design was published which then officially separated fine arts from graphic designing. The term 'Graphic Design' was coined after the publication of Raffe's book Graphic Design (1927)."1

Graphic design, is a necessary niche intertwined with the online world and in the world of sight. Our vision is what allows us to step forward, to dream, to imagine, before we are prompted to take action. Sight is utmost important and every successful graphic designer knows this, or will begin to realize this fact.

When thinking about graphic design, a non graphic artist often thinks solely about logos. Yet logos aren't everything when it comes to graphic design. But do keep in mind, graphic design is essential for logos to even exist. Design, art and innovation are both in the world of graphics. The nicer and more cutting edge, the better.

Graphic artists always need to step up their game when competing with other graphic artists. Graphic design is a skill that is greatly in demand and something that the market needs. Graphic designers are a dime a dozen. Graphic designers have the ability to work from home or in a company office, it all depends on the preference that the designer has. Some graphic artists make menial compensation while others can make grand compensation.All graphic artists have the ability to pick and choose their clients once they are established. So pick projects that are good for you once you are at this point. As long as the designers portfolio work is good enough and well established, and the designer is able to provide the client with great references, the graphic artists life will become easier and less stressful. Clients love professionalism and value someone who is established.

Since there are different types of graphic designs used for many purposes, there is a plausible reason to list them all. All readers continue along for the purposes and benefits directly related to the world of graphic design. Graphic design isn't only utilized for logos, the skill is used for all types of business purposes that deal with, but is not limited to: marketing, filmmaking, news, media, retail, business cards, print, you name it, every single sector purchases graphic design at one point or another.

Graphic designers are the starters and the beginners of companies and brands. Just think about it. Before a C.E.O gets started with opening up their business, who do they consult with? A designer, a graphic designer. They need a logo, company name, and a summary of their business, among many other things. In an essence this makes you the creator of designing a beginning brand, empowering the designer to the title: The Alpha, well, every graphic designer would sure like to think that of themselves, and they should.

Design with all of your heart, as these designs and logos are almost engraved into society through decades or hundreds of years perhaps. The designs that are created can make or break a reputation, a value, or a belief.

According to payscale.com the job description of a graphic designer is described as, "Graphic designers use color, illustrations, fonts, and layout to visually communicate a message or present a product. They design logos, product packaging, print materials, and websites, among many other things. Graphic designers are found in a variety of industries and in different capacities. For instance, a designer might be employed as in-house staff for a company to work on promotional materials for the organization, or a designer might work for a design agency with many clients and projects.

Newspapers, advertising firms, technology-oriented companies, and other organizations commonly employ designers. Additionally, many graphic designers are self- employed, working as independent contractors on a per-project basis."

Graphic Designer Tasks Include:

- Design and develop product brand identity.
- Direct marketing design projects, collaborating with multiple departments.
- Create and assemble images and graphics to produce designs for websites, print media, product design,

displays and productions."

Branding

Proper branding is what sells a product. Brands are not only ideas, brands are the entire representation of the product and service trying to increase and obtain profit in the economy. Graphic designers are some of the masterminds behind any company branding.

Lets take Starbucks as an example. There is a mermaid woman with a crown and a star on her head, she has long hair, and has a background color of green, white, and black. The alluring female is wearing a crown and appears simplistic yet royalist. The logo is very inviting and has been described as looking elite. Mixing coffee and a mermaid has proven to be pure profitable excellence over the years. The designer helped Starbucks attain this type of look through the graphical design and look of the logo. The logo is balanced, and the star on her head draws the consumer in.

Starbucks was founded in Seattle Washington on March 30, 1971. Entrepreneur.com makes a valid statement about branding: "Branding is one of the most important aspects of any business, large or small, retail or B2B. An effective brand strategy gives you a major edge in increasingly competitive markets. But what exactly does "branding" mean? How does it affect a small business like yours? "Simply put, your brand is your promise to your customer. It tells them what they can expect from your products and services, and it differentiates your offering from your competitors'. Your brand is derived from who you are, who you want to be and who people perceive you to be." (entreprenuer.com).

Business Prospect- The Technical Age

Graphic design is represented by many freelancers and contracted employees. In fact, there are plenty of graphic designers who will have a career and do graphic design on the side in order to supplement their income for pure hobby. Graphic design basically entails a lot of visualization, pure creativity, and technical skills. Many professional individuals usually fall into this niche simply because they have found a hobby within the world of graphic design.

Of course, there is a lot of money to be made with anything that becomes a high demand. Graphic design is, in fact highly in demand in our world today. Many clients and business owners do recognize the importance of their brand and this is where graphic design comes in.

As the company grows in size and reputation, graphic design becomes essential, providing ongoing business for the graphic designer.

Customers view and buy with their eyes, this is why it is important to delve into the world of graphic design, if technological design is your forte. Not only can an artist change the way reality looks with graphic design, but with the technical software that is now offered on the market, it enables for great visual and interactive effects.

Graphic designers and artists have tools to go as far as three dimensions now. Cartoons can now be created on a computer and so can movement. Digital artists have so many tools to work with. It is definitely possible to make a six figure salary. Especially if the graphic designer sets their own prices, and only if the graphic artist has a lot of clientele and sets their prices and time at a high value.

Having a well established portfolio is a must before any job postings and proposals become accepted. All graphic designers need to be prepared to face a lot of competition. This also forces each designer to have eye popping art that is better than the ones of the next man or woman who wants the job.

It is essentially about the art as a whole, but as with any industry, the professional working individual needs to have a likable personality - clients want to work with people they like and want to work with. Having interpersonal communication skills will therefor get you a long way and will definitely ensure that you get a leg up.

The great thing about the graphic design career is that after a well established reputation has been set in place, the graphic design artist can work wherever he or she prefers, even from his or her own bed, if one really wanted to.

https://flic.kr/p/wrhM83

The key is to be creative, innovative and to know the software which you will be working on. Know the software in and out, have a splendid portfolio, hone interpersonal communication skills; this is an absolute must. Lastly, keep in mind that persistence and self-motivation are absolute necessities in order to succeed and survive in this computational and creative world of graphic design.

Typical Graphic Designer Salary, Don't Stay Typical

Here is the fun part, the salary. The average salary of a company graphic designer reaches around, $48,500.00 - $50,000.00 annually. There are some graphic designers who have exceeded these amounts by far with higher amounts per year. Higher profits should always be strived for by the graphic designer who is climbing the ropes.

A beginning graphic designer may get as little as $15.00 an hour, so hurry up and build an eye catching portfolio. Don't be a late bird, the saying always sticks, "the early bird catches the worm". Be sure to seek higher and more established clients with newly profitable brands or already established brands. Avoid $15.00 an hour, that treatment should no longer have to be endured. It is true though, all graphic designers have to start somewhere.

Payout

Freelance and independent contracted employees can make as much as they set their goals to. A higher salary depends on how much the freelancers perseverance and dedication can withstand the myriads of projects thrown into their computers at once, or the proposals being rejected.

As a freelancer, the stress is on. Anyone's quality of life can be immediately changed depending on what career path they choose. An artist needs to prove their value to the professional world, and with growing value comes a more prosperous future.

A Techy Industry

Any new graphic designer must enjoy the technology sector. The newest gadgets and technology gizmos will most likely give every graphic designer an advantage, as they can be used as tools for art creation. Gizmos and technology gadgets sure can't cover up a bad design though. Every graphic designer needs to love computers as they are gifts to all artistic and digital designers.

The tech sector is thriving, and so is the entertainment industry. In the big picture, our economy is drowning. The fact that these sectors are the ones surviving, should be the first tell tale sign that graphic designers are more sought after in the year 2015. The entertainment industry seeks designers on a constant basis as the public lives on entertainment.

Web designers on the other hand are also highly needed as we have entered the era of the digital and data age. Data is overflowing and this fact gives the best graphic artists a chance to stand out. Facebook has created a world of likes. If a graphic artist can create a million likes, work and sponsors will follow. People can't live without their smartphones, their iPads, their Apple computers, etc. The population has become reliant yet addicted to the digital age, our computers.

Graphic designers are set forth to feed the hungry public with our creation of individual visualizations through multi-media and graphics. The way in which we work has changed. Data, brands, products, and capital are being tossed into billions of hands each day, each second. Graphic designers are essential to economic growth and future visualization. Staying techy and «in the now» as a graphic designer will advantage the creator with a prosperous and comfortable lifestyle down the road.

Constantly educating and improving ones illustrating skills will also prevail, as many artists struggle when it comes to cartoons.

Take a long running, 574 episode cartoon for example. The Simpsons. The creator Matt Groening submitted illustrations for the cartoon family, Homer, Marge, Lisa, Bart, and Maggie Simpson, soon after they became digitized with an illustrative appeal. Matt Groening drew the images, making him the creator and the graphic designer. The creator, Matt Groening's imagination coupled with his ability to create something where he saw a gap in the market worked. According to celebritynetworth.com Matt Groening has been able to accumulate a 500 million net worth! So when speaking about compensation, graphic designers and creators all have future hope to make well above $50,000 a year. Graphic designers need to keep thinking outside the box, they need to not only create, but all graphic designers need to focus on keeping and earning higher profits.

Set Your Own Rules

As a freelancer, a contractor, or even a company hired employee, you must always set professional rules and standards for yourself and stick to your word. It is true if you don't have your word, then you pretty much don't have anything. Stick firmly to your word and make sure to set a goal before you even start talking to prospective clients.

When you are seeking out projects you must first decide on what type of clients you are seeking out. Then you have to decide on the slowest price you are willing to go down to. Of course the price of the project will vary depending on each individual project. Choose your projects wisely before you begin the creation endeavor of creating new graphic designs for a new client. Make sure you raise any questions that you may have about the project to the client.

It is true, if you are going to start something, one must know their craft from the inside and out. Keep practicing for ongoing perfection. If you standardize rules, clients can not impede on your professional standards. Some may try, but being a freelancer and independent contractor can sure propel every successful graphic designer to the next level.

It is important to know that some clients will do their very best to try to take control over the freelancer. You can easily prevent this from happening by making your own contract to protect yourself. This contract/ template that states your professional working rules is easier to hand away then restating your rules time and time again. Make a documented contract to cover yourself in case something inevitable comes up along the way. Life and business is precarious, protect yourself against getting taken advantage of, and most importantly protect yourself against possible infringement or stealing of one's images/ intellectual property.

Make sure you get paid for your work. Know your rights, your rules, your standards, and professionally carry on into the abyss of high success within this special known niche of graphic design. Sit down and take your graphic design brain out for one second, think business and begin to think how you will protect your work and your payment. Get a contract that stipulates these elements, so the client can see your terms in plain old English. It is always easy to set a guideline of rules. Stick to your own rules. Every single graphic designer needs to set-up an hourly wage or fixed price depending on the project, there is always room to negotiate with clients, so be sure not to eradicate this idea.

https://flic.kr/p/7yAJjG

Competitive Candidates

The great thing about being a graphic designer is that the artist has plenty of avenues and routes to chose from. A graphic designer must not feel embossed, for the mere fact that there are plenty of choices when it comes to a position or a project. Finding your niche is one thing, but once you know what you want to do, there is a niche within a niche to be found.

New job positions are needed and open up all of the time. With our ever-changing ways involved with the rapid increase of the internet, population growth, regions that are under developed, and technology, there is enormous room for intellectual growth in the field of graphic design. Graphic design is used to convey an appetizing message to the viewer via artistic elements and composition. The idea of graphic design is derived from the print industry. Through technology a myriad of new positions sky rocketed and became available.

Clients are always looking for the best graphic designers. Usually when applying to the highest paid projects, it is always good to show clients work that you did for clients previously. Names are everything in the world of graphic design.

Take the Apple logo for instance. The designer sure did make quite a reputable logo. People from all around see and love the brand. It is the graphic designers job to visually please all eyes that are looking. Seminars and extra classes are available to students looking to improve their hand at this craft. Be sure to stay 'in the know,' when it comes to art, especially new media art as the younger generation is constantly learning new and better ways of creation.

Being in a state of constantly learning will keep every graphic designer prime and youthful on their feet. Being in the graphic design industry will enable stable and monetary success for the artist. Stay competitive and constantly learn in order to win the bid.

Types of Graphic Design

With the world becoming more and more innovative and individuals beginning thinking outside the box, there are plenty of new types of graphic design that are starting to appear in all types of industries. As stated previously, graphic design and logos originated from the print industry. Logos, posters, company designs, flyers, direct mailers, websites, brochures, cereal boxes, movie posters, you name it, some artist did design it.

Some graphic designers use photography and then distort this new media project on software such as Photoshop, Illustrator, etc. Since we are not necessarily speaking about a sketch artist, one main requirement for a graphic designer is to become equipped with a computer and the proper cutting edge software. It is learning the short cuts and the in's and out's of the software that will help a graphic designer the most.

Deciding to Have a Career in Graphic Design

If you want to free your creativity and pursue your craft in order to make a happy living, start by gaining all the knowledge you can possibly get your eyes on! Read, observe, and retain. When a person decides they want to become a graphic designer, they must be willing to not only put in the grueling hours and edits, but they must keep in mind that they need to decide whether or not they want to go corporate or stay freelance.

One good thing about graphic design is that it is a skill. So even if you are an individual who isn't set on your particular career path, then it is still wise to proceed with learning about this craft, as it can prove to be a valuable fall back for part-time work or for pleasure. Graphic design is very fluid as there is not always a set schedule. This is especially true if you work for yourself, in this case, an individual finds their projects on their own terms - making this position an alternative and a supplement income for the household.

Independent Contractor Vs. Corporate Employee

Every route has its pros and cons. Independent contractors have the luxury of working under their own terms, deciding their income, project by project, hour by hour. All freelance graphic artists have a lot of freedom. This is certainly a great perk that you will get when working for yourself. If stagnancy and sitting still is not on your agenda, then motivate yourself and make your own profit, become a freelancer. Work for yourself.

One of the downsides, if you chose to go the freelancer route is that you have to purchase your own healthcare, IRA, and extra stocks/investments. There is no company to pay those benefits, you, the freelancer, are the company.

When it comes to graphic design and working on the corporate side of things, an employee is usually cut at a certain max salary. There is no movement for growth, leaving the graphic artist with a stagnant salary. But, you have to keep in mind the value of always having a recurrent paycheck. This may give you, the artist peace of mind.

The Sky Is Always The Limit

Just like any true artist, gaining creative recognition is critically important for any artist. Who doesn't want to be known for their talents? Make therefor sure to keep your eyes closely glued to the screen while you create on Photoshop, Illustrator, or whichever software you may be using. It is true, if any individual has a deep rooted passion, then reaching for the stars has to be and is the answer.

Every graphic designer needs to keep in mind that they will not be awarded every single project that they apply for. The market is extremely competitive. The wisdom to take away from this is not to get your hopes down and don't stop trying when rejection seems heavy. The thing every graphic designer needs, is to keep a cool head and logically apply to projects that he or she can complete with not only magnificent articulation, grace, and style, but with their 110% effort put forth. Do an amazing job and you may end up gaining a repetitious and longterm professional client. Adding new clients will not only increase your funds, but it will overall increase your portfolio that should always be on hand and ready for show.

Creativity and Spice

Ok, enough about the business aspect of being a graphic artist. Lets get into the nitty gritty of design. Graphic design is 100% artistic because each and every graphic designer uses their complete creative nature when it comes to graphics design and art. Although most artists thrive better when they create their own pieces of work, their own masterpieces, if the client has a certain vision, you, the graphic designer must put your own creativity aside and follow their vision. You can still add your own visual touch, but hear and listen to what they want.

As long as you follow the directions set forth by your client you can add your creative spark to the logo or graphic. Just keep in mind that edits are the norm. Completing a project the way a client wants should be every graphic designers utmost concern.

be an amateur. Creating logos for websites, videos, promos and the web in general is a technical skill, so be sure to take some necessary workshops before you decide to delve into the position with full force. Every graphic designer who wants to get better and better with the creation of their own designs should never feel limited, using imagination and then computerization will keep ideas fresh and interesting.

Information Architect

It is important to keep in mind that graphic designer do not only make illustrations. Graphic designers also design text. The position - Information Architect has been created due to the increase of data being transferred into everyones screens, eyes, and brains on regular basis. The salary of a graphic designer in the position, 'Manager Information Architect' topples around six figures!

Every graphic designer needs to decide how they want to use their creativity and intellectualism. Some designers need more color and humor in their lives, like Matt Groening, the creator of The

Simpsons. While other graphic designers enjoy organizing data, to make it more recognizable, securable, and understandable to the human eye. An Information Architect according to salary.com makes around $143,000 annually.

Film Industry Graphics

The film industry is a great industry to work in, minus the grueling normal twelve hour days. In the film industry the hours might be grueling, you may be on call, but depending on what project you are working on and how it explodes in popularity, you might be compensated pretty well. If you are involved in a project like the AMC television show, 'Breaking Bad', you as a graphic designer will gain serious street and professional credits.

When the designer applies to their next gig, having a project with such a popular name will almost be sure to get the designer the job over the other guy. Test your skills and abilities, seek out higher paying projects with bigger names, and your bank account will eventually thank you.

Always remember, once you land the project, do a 110% job. Soon clients with open projects will flock to your credible and reputable name that you have built. It may be a bit hard to enter the film industry as it is very small, but having the right friend, family member, or perseverance and dedication will be sure to get you into this new and entertaining arena of graphic design. Be sure to consider yourself a freelancer or contractor at this point as your pay per project would be higher than a salary. Make sure to document every hour you work, as a beginner in the film industry, a naive designer could get taken advantage of, don't let it happen to you. Word of advice, take heed, never trust anyone's word in this industry unless there is signed paperwork with ink.

Company/Commercial

Being a graphic designer for a normal company who produces commercial creative content is another option for graphic designers. Graphic designers are hired to produce designs, logos, poster material, images, etc. The projects pay per the hour or per project depending on the client. Everyone in the commercial industry is aware that the pay is greater than most other jobs. Graphic designers that design for commercials make a decent amount of money per year.

Mac Vs. PC

When it comes to technology and computers, this questions always seems to arise one way or another - it is inevitable. Which computer is better, Mac or a PC? The answer is, knowing both systems is proven to be more advantageous to the graphic designer for the mere fact that each client is different. It is important to be informed and in-the-know about both computer system. As a graphic designer your job is to know the technicality behind the digital world, computers in general. Keep yourself not only up-to-date, but keep yourself knowledgable about everything clients are using, including all computer systems.

Print Advertising

Ah the glory of print. This is where the industry of graphic design started in its youthful prime. Every graphic designer has the ability to stay flexible with their time. Usually print companies now outsource for graphic designers instead of paying them and giving them an in-house salary. This sounds as if it doesn't work in the favor of the graphic designer, as print companies and other companies these days have limited the amount of positions they post for graphic design jobs. This is merely because print companies started suffering once the advent of the internet decided to hit all time highs. Uploading images is as easy as a click. Having flexibility and doing 'side' projects for print companies can boost anyones income. Don't stay stuck with a nine to five. Venture out, trust in yourself, obtain the work, and prove your worth!

Visualizing a Design

Congrats to all graphic designers who wrote a great proposal, had top-notch samples of work for their clients to review, sold yourself to the client, and landed the project. The hard part is now over. You, the artist, can now ease yourself into the creative mindset of graphic design. Now that the first step is surpassed you can now move on to the next step: creative visualization. Before any graphic artist starts out, make sure to know just exactly what your client is looking for. Know your clients wishes from the bottom to the top. Don't miss any minor details, as it could stunt your professionalism soon after.

Make sure to ask any questions that you may have, and know what you are working with in order to increase your chances on pinpointing the clients goals from the get go. Stay confident, but listen intently. Visually speaking, a graphic artist should be able to compose a high end piece, using brushes, paint, shapes, filters, and text within the software.

Let's go for a global sample, the Nike logo. The Nike logo is known everywhere. The check is pristine yet very simple. As long as you have a creative brain coming up with the design, then the physical work is simple. Sit back, enjoy your computer, your imagination, and design.

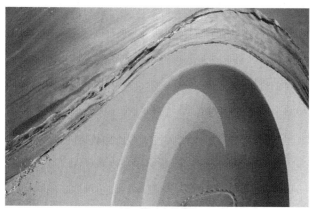

Creative Collaboration

When it comes to creative collaboration, before the start of creation, make sure that the client is always present via phone or internet because you, the graphic designer, will have questions regarding your newly awarded project.

The types of questions that you will need to ask all depends on what the client has already presented to you. If you need to know if certain restrictions follow the design, be sure to listen to the clients wants and needs. Ask any questions if there happens to be any confusion or gaps in your ideas. Get an idea about what the mission of the company is. Also answers question like, What does the company believe in? What are the companies values and goals? What targets does the company have, who are they targeting? These are good indications about how a graphic design should be articulated. Once the designer has been given the appropriate information, a perfect envisioned design can begin to develop.

The Process

Everything and anything notable takes an entire process. Start with a goal, make a plan, create, execute, and touch-up. That is the motto in this precarious yet exciting industry of graphic design.

First decide on what type of graphic design that you are going to create. Once you have an idea and know the tools you will need to get started, you can begin.

If you are going to need a picture, make sure to have photography skills, or make sure to pay for a copyrighted photo and get the right kind of approval before moving forward. If you decide that you will only need your brain and the computer, then you are all set and ready to design.

Open Adobe Illustrator or Photoshop, whichever you feel the most comfortable with and choose the tools you will need. Then start following the guidelines that were given to you regarding the project, if you have any. Your goal as a graphic designer is to make sure the composition of the design is what the client is looking for. The composition is dealing with: size, color, shapes, aesthetics based toward the human eye, etc.

Make sure your eyes are keen and that your attention to detail is up to par. This will enable a clean and accomplished graphic. Starting with the basics, remember to follow your guidelines. Using Adobe software will aide every graphic designer to perform at their max. Keep in mind that, sometimes mistakes turn into something good especially during any creation process.

Styles, Fonts, Designs, Shapes, and Filters

When it comes to graphic design, the designing doesn't seem to get boring as a graphic designer who actually appreciates his or her own craft is able to do loads of creative endeavors with the use of technology, tools, and software.

Using different fonts compiled with images and color contrast is sure to create an effect. Distorting an image and making it appear backwards can also create some type of emotional response when a consumer or viewer comes across the graphic.

Computer applications enable designers to play with lighting, space, color, and design. These aspects that are involved in the creation of graphic design are imminent as they are what brings the entire design to life.

Psychology Behind The Design

As a graphic designer, please keep in mind that there will be plenty of people viewing your logo and or design at one point or another. Make sure to use your best judgment when it comes to creating a top-notch and professional graphic. When speaking about the psychology behind the design, here is some food for thought.

There has been plenty of research done on fast food restaurants and their logos. McDonald's and plenty of large scale fast food companies tend to use the colors, yellow and red. After doing plenty of research, there has been public results stating that these colors are known to increase a customers appetite.

Pleasant colors like blue present warmness and a calm nature, while black can present as classic and clean feeling. The color red can present pure dominance. There are many theories about color and logos. It is in every designers best interest to delve into more individual research not just with colors, but try numbers and shapes, as these elements as a whole will help the graphic designer create a successful logo.

A Beginning Walk Through: Photoshop

Before purchasing this software, make sure to test out the free trial that Abode offers to customers on their website at http://www.adobe.com. Make sure that you are set on making this investment towards your future goals of entering and being a graphic designer. It is true, all artists are unique and all individuals learn differently than others.

Some graphic artists learn purely by experimenting on the system and by clicking around. But it is highly advised to look further into the aspect of digital design as there are many tricks and short cuts that aide every graphic designer with utmost efficiency. Obtaining more knowledge and educating yourself about the intricacy of the software will allow you to make designs you have never thought you could digitally create. Who knows, maybe you will create something that the market dreams of seeing. In such a case, you, the graphic designer, will soon have other clients flocking to your artistic ability.

A Beginning Walk Through: Illustrator

Adobe Illustrator has different effects compared to AdobePhotoshop. Adobe photoshop allows for text, graphics, picture fix and distort, etc, while Illustrator offers more precise tools for an actual illustrator.

Media is an industry that can make or break someone. Tap into this market as a graphic designer and you just may follow in the footsteps of Matt Groening, The Simpson's cartoon creator, and now multi-millionaire. Many cartoon designs later become classic hits.

Take the MTV production that was popular at the early part of the twentieth century, Daria. An Illustrator created Daria, which was then sold to MTV. The show is brilliantly witty. There is a lot of room to flourish when it comes to the ongoing and ever changing world of digital arts and cartoons.

Video Game Graphic Designers

Graphic designers are creating designs for this interactive media. Graphic designers salary who design specifically for video games can make close to $100,000 a year, according to payscale.com. The designer must know Adobe Photoshop and Illustrator inside and out in order to begin creating a video game design.

The job can be exciting, interesting, challenging, and exhausting. Graphic designers are getting better and better at creating designs, as the designs appear to look too real. People become addicted to video games for the fact that video games are so entertaining and real-life-like. The game becomes somewhat of a reality, a suspension of disbelief. So in a sense, the graphic designer of the video game is kind of similar to a creator, an art director, a director or a producer.

Graphic designers have plenty of avenues to take when it comes to job seeking. There is a variety of positions always needed and opening in the graphic arts industry. It is up the the designer to find their niche. After that they must actually be good at it, or success will not follow suit.

Web Design & HTML + HTML 5

Web design is kind of like owning a piece of real estate, except the real estate is intellectual property and the content and visual design is located on the internet. The internet is a place for the whole entire public to see, read and share data and information. Not only can people access content via their smartphones, desktop, and iPad's, but they can make up their minds about a product or brand.

If the website content proves to look aesthetically poor, then possible business could become immediately and forever lost. Dreadful scenarios like this happen all too often, this is why professional graphic designers exist. Someone who knows how to build and maintain a website and someone who knows about the elements and composition about building a catching and moving brand.

These are important skills that all achieving graphic designers must have in order to progress forward. Graphic designers love working on website projects, as these projects seem to be ongoing and repetitious, as long as the client is benefiting from the website. Getting products known and into the consumers eyes and homes is every C.E.O's challenge and dream. Paying for a professional graphic designer to build a website that allures buyers and enables effective efficiency for the consumer, will always prevail against any testy drab and non useful website.

We have all come across amateur websites and they are not too shiny. When a graphic designer accepts such a project, he or she can make thousands of dollars in a matter of days. Simply by honing this technical yet creative skill allows the graphic designer to deposit quick money into his or her bank. This skill not only comes in handy, but is handy when the graphic designer markets hisself or herself heavily. Simple HTML skills are needed to build a website, but it is always recommended that graphic designers stay on top of the newest software and technological jargon, and trends. This will aide graphic designers in the ever-changing competitive designing market. Sure it is good to know the basics in the computer world, but let's move past the basics for now. Graphic designers are hired because they can solve a complication with visual and graphical description and satiation.

Knowing Flash

We have all heard about Adobe Flash one way or another. A well paid graphic designer better get well aquatinted with this type of software application. Doing so will prove to pay off, and in some cases this skill is necessary in order to become qualified for an interview in the first place. Knowing more information will always be in favor for every trying professional. Flash is used mostly for animation type purposes, yet some clients will look baffled and look down upon anyone who calls themselves a graphic designer yet doesn't know a single thing about Adobe Flash. As a graphic designer, learning to build projects and applications will be an advantage for the graphic designer.

It is important to maintain a fierce set of skills to stay active in the designing market. There are many websites on the internet that take advantage of Flash, most clients want options, so make sure to keep your skill-set wide. Flash should be in your back pocket or in a graphic designers case, installed in ones computer device.

Adobe Flash gives graphic designers the ability to work frame by frame, giving flash an advantage over the regular use of html. With frame by frame, graphic designers can use vector shapes, video, and animation all-in-one. This enables them to create designs that top other artists. As long as true creativity exists and the technicality behind the software is discovered, efficiently learned and implemented, the artistic possibilities are wide and range far beyond.

Distortion

There are many fun and interesting tools in the Adobe Illustrator application and on any design software. Here is a task. Take a photo of something you want, upload it, then open it in Adobe Photoshop, click on filters, scroll down to the distort option. Once you do this your image will be distorted, the changes will then be seen. Change the lighting, add some text. The new image could very well look like a movie poster now. There are plenty of experiments to be had on the distortion option. Distortion causes projects to look a bit mysterious, depending on the image.

Graphic Designer! Market Yourself Avidly

Every graphic designer is always marketing for their clients and making their clients appear better and more professional with an artistic and graphic appeal. What every graphic designer needs to keep in mind though, is to not forget about themselves.

Working on everyone else's project while making money can surely cause any graphic designer to forget about themselves in the short and long- run. Don't forget to make sure that you, the graphic designer, constantly updates your own website with newer innovations in order to repetitiously attract future clients and professional allies. Market and share your work online. Research and find forums and groups. The saying, it is all about who you know, still lies true in this industry.

Branch out and meet others who are in need of graphic designers. Reach out to other artists, show your work, attend events, be friendly, and always ask for recommendations to further your career. Recommendations are sure to get you your next job. You, the graphic designer, needs to keep all of your websites, your resume, your clientele (if you choose to disclose), your portfolio, LinkedIn, not only up-to-date, but enticing and inviting to all readers.

If you neglect these simple marketing tactics, your name wont be able to get a firm grip and hold in the marketplace. Don't make the mistake of appearing as an amateur online. That is the worst thing any graphic designer can do. Nurture your online appearance and be sure to Google your name and make sure all of the information regarding you is relevant.

Be aware of your name, reputation, and what online data has stored for you, the graphic designer, who is looking for more work. Make sure your name and or graphic design company is not only reputable and credible, but is presented well. It is true, presentation is everything. Any professional graphic designer can attest to this statement. Make sure your overall reputation is pristine and honorable as it will get you higher paying clients. It is essential to work on your own brand first and foremost before working on everyone else's brand.

Attending Workshops

Here is another important lesson to all graphic designers that coexist in this world: Research and keep up with the latest happenings around your community and around the world globally. Not only will attending graphic design workshops and lectures enhance your intellectual strength and power, but it will increase the amount of individuals that know who you are.

Emerge yourself from solo seclusion that the stereotypical graphic designer prefers, and get out there and meet like- minded people to improve the amount of business that comes your way. Some good sites can be easily found on our handy search engine, Google.

There is competition, so make sure to knock on a lot of doors, because it is likely that no one is directly going to knock on your door (especially if your name isn't already out there).

Upon Finish

There are important factors to keep in mind as a graphic designer. One, always learn and improve your skills. Secondly, become a good listener. Third, your portfolio must be great!

Hobby Meets Modern Day Politics

Art is a powerful tool and by now, one would think, every educated and even non-educated individual can determine this statement and mark it as valid. Art is subjective, and can and has caused political controversy since the beginning of time. Art continues to change, shape, and educate or skew individuals around. Anyone striving to be a true graphic designer should know that their artwork can, in fact shape plenty of political factors. It is therefor important to use design and graphical content with complete and open awareness and high consciousness.

From spray painted graffiti, to pin-point sketches, paintings, you name it, it can become digital. Graphic artists have many capabilities and tools they can utilize when creating a design. Their limitations are small and their successes and abilities are grand.

New Media Emergence

Computer design, image manipulation, and visual transformation pertains to new media. New media has been around for awhile, but the emergence of the newly found niche didn't take on full notice until the internet gained it's popularity in the eighties and nineties.

New artists and graphic designers soon became discovered, for their new type of art. Since the emergence of new media, new jobs have been created, new classes have opened, new artists have been mentioned, and new awareness has been created. In a nutshell, new media consists of art that is put onto a computer device and tweaked around with.

An example would be making a collage on paper, scanning the document, and distorting the art piece via Photoshop. New Media is referred to as anything newly interconnected with the internet and technological devices. Graphic designers who know how to do in-depth new media projects are highly in demand. This is due to the fact that data and information is constantly needed to be seen by the public on an everyday basis.

Well- Known Graphic Designers

New York City is one of the most populous cities in the United States of America. It is no wonder that our global economy considers New York City the center of the universe! The logo I HEART NY (constructed with an actual heart shape) is famous. The Heart and simplicity of the logo is known and bought by many tourists and locals. The man behind the logo is graphic designer Milton Glaser.

This is a list of graphic designers that every graphic designer should know of. Please see the list below and take a look at the names and exactly what they specialized in. Not only will you learn new methods, ideas, and perspectives, but you will also get to see the difference between past and modern graphic art. The changes are enormous. The great changes are to a great extend caused by the quick entry of the internet and new and more powerful computer technology.

The graphic designers below have climbed the ranks and have become successful as a result of designs that they have created. Each artist occupies their own niche within graphic design.

1. Otl Aicher

"Good art inspires; Good design motivates."

Nationality: German

Studied at: Academy of Fine Arts Munich

Era active: 1940s through 1980s

Specialties: Identity, typography

Known for: Lufthansa branding, 1972 Munich Olympics, Ulm School of Design

2. Michael Beirut

"Only good work leads to doing more good work."

Nationality: American

Studied at: University of Cincinnati's College of Design, Architecture, Art and Planning

Era active: 1980s through present

Specialties: Identity and print work, design writing and criticism

Known for: Redesign of The Atlantic, graphics for the New York Times building

3. Neville Brody

"Design is more than just a few tricks to the eye. It's a few tricks to the brain."

Nationality: British

Studied at: London College of Printing

Era active: 1970s to present

Specialties: Typography, art direction

Known for: The Face Magazine, Arena Magazine, record cover art

4. David Carson

"Graphic design will save the world right after rock and roll does."

Nationality: American
Studied at: Oregon College of Commercial Art
Era active: 1980s through present
Specialties: Magazine design, art direction
Known for: Ray Gun Magazine

5. Alan Fletcher

"I like to reduce everything to its absolute

essence because that is a way to avoid getting trapped in a style."

Nationality: British
Studied at: Hammersmith School of Art, Central School of Art, Royal College of Art, Yale School of Architecture
Era active: 1960s – 1990s
Specialties: Identity design, book design
Known for: Founding Partner of Pentagram, The Art of Looking Sideways

6. Chip Kidd

"Never fall in love with an idea. They're whores: if the one you're with isn't doing the job, there's always, always, always another."

Nationality: American

Studied at: Pennsylvania State University

Era active: 1980s through present

Specialties: Book cover design

Known for: So many awesome book covers and his work with graphic novels

7. Armin Hofmann

"There should be no separation between spontaneous work with an emotional tone and work directed by the intellect. Both are supplementary to each other and must be regarded as intimately connected. Discipline and freedom are thus to be seen as elements of equal weight, each partaking of the other."

Nationality: Swiss

Studied at: Apprenticed in lithography

Era active: 1940s through 1980s

Specialties: Poster design

Known for: His teachings as head of Schule für Gestaltung Basel, poster for Giselle

8. Herb Lubalin

"You can do a good ad without good typography, but you can't do a great ad without good typography."

Nationality: American

Studied at: Cooper Union

Era active: 1940s through 1980s

Specialties: Typography, art direction

Known for: ITC Avant Garde font, work on Eros and Avant Garde magazines

9. Stefan Sagmeister

"It is very important to embrace failure and to do a lot of stuff — as much stuff as possible — with as little fear as possible. It's much, much better to wind up with a lot of crap having tried it than to overthink in the beginning and not do it.

Nationality: Austrian

Studied at: University of Applied Arts Vienna, Pratt Institute

Era active: 1990s through present

Specialties: Album covers, typography

Known for: Lou Reed Poster, book Things I have learned in my life so far

10. Paula Scher

"You never can do what the kids do. What you do is look at yourself and find your own way to address the fact that the times have changed and that you have to pay attention. You can't be a designer and say, 'Oh, this is timeless.' Nothing is timeless!"

Nationality: American
Studied at: Tyler School of Art
Era active: 1970s through present
Specialties: Branding and identity, album covers, illustration

Known for: Her poster work, and being the first female principal at Pentagram

Education

All graphic designers need some type of schooling whether it is formal schooling or a workshop to learn about Flash, HTML, Illustrator, Photoshop, you name it.

Rejection in the world of design happens all of the time, it is true. Take this lightly, as rejection comes along, it is the name of the game. Art is subjective and everyone buying and appreciating art and design is different. Graphic designers need to realize this - everyone needs to. As stated before, it is in every graphic designers best interest to have schooling backing their amazing portfolio. It will only add future security to any designers lifelong career of digital design. When a graphic artist is in the midst of their career and is already established, it can't be stressed enough how important it is for you to showcase only your best work in your graphic artist portfolio. Sub par work will not qualify, so make sure to clean out your portfolio and include about five to ten pieces of your best work.

Education is expensive, and if it was easy, everyone would attend and finish. This is not the case by any means. Every graphic designer should take some kind of seminar or class to not only learn more, but for mere experience and intellectual socialization. Every time a new perspective or idea is mentioned to anyone, especially to artists like graphic designers, it enables the graphic artist to think outside of their current thoughts and ideas. This will ultimately have an effect on the art work created.

Seminars that teach a more in-depth approach to producing graphic art is a great for learning the technical concepts behind certain software and computerizations. Seminars and workshops are something worth saving up for. It is a good investment for every graphic designer looking to create more efficiency with technicality or simply wanting to learn newer ideas and concepts. The cost of seminars and workshops can be considered fairly reasonable as every graphic designer who practices their craft can get their investment back multiple times. Receiving this kind of education usually creates an enormous amount of efficiency and effectiveness.

The pros about receiving seminar/ workshop schooling over a four year Computer Sciences degree, is that the graphic designer will have more time to design for a living rather than for a grade. Either way, any kind of schooling an individual can get their hands on should be their first priority. Education can not be stressed enough. Go on, gain a new perspective, look outside your own box, design, and make your education investment money turn to profitable money.

Knowledge is known to bring power. Every successful graphic designer not only has to think like an artist, but every graphic artist also needs to think like a business man or woman. Education will prime anyone for the professionalism they will need in the real world. Designing for the love of the craft is a given and graphic designers should never forget why they started designing in the first place. Always remember your skills are very valuable, and your time is worth monetary value. Even artists and designers have to survive, so educate yourself as much as you possibly can.

Schools Specializing in Graphic Design

To take the leg work out for all graphic designers reading this, here is a list of schools that specialize in the education of graphic design. The top ten graphic design schools according to U.S. news grad-schools, ranking and reviews.com are:

I.   Rhode Island School of Design
II. Yale University
III. Maryland Institute College of Art
IV. Carnegie Mellon University
V.   Virginia Commonwealth University
VI. Cranbrook Academy of Art
VII. Art Center College of Design

These Universities are well known in the industry of graphic design. New artists are emerging every semester. Although some artist's don't necessarily need a college degree to be successful and good, a University is a great place for learning about the world in a global sense. Education should always be a top priority, no matter what. There have been studies stating that college graduates do in fact make more money than a high school graduate. The fact is proven to be true. So study up and save up.

Mindset

If you haven't got the right «design mindset» yet, following the simple guidelines below will be sure to aide any designers block. All artists are stumped at one point or another, so it is relevant to step back and listen. Getting into the mindset of creating can come to some people so easily, while other designers have a hard time getting 'in the zone'. Go ahead, sit back and relax.

Stress can take a large chunk of energy from a person. Therefor try to minimize your stress before you begin any project. It sounds counterintuitive for the fact that projects and work are most likely to bring about the physical and mental feeling of stress. It doesn't have to be that way. There are ways to use design as a meditation and a relaxing experiment. So here it goes. First things first, minimize all stress, noise, and distraction. Sit in a comfortable work space and make sure that you are sitting upright in a proper seated position with your spine straight. It is smart to buy an ergonomics friendly keyboard and mouse, because as a graphic designer, you will be required to sit for long periods of time.

As a graphic designer, the key is not only getting into a comfortable mindset for design, the key is properly using your physical self when you are at the computer for long periods of time. Take deep breathes and do some stretches before you start the creation process. Make sure that you have a clean work space and that you eat properly. The human body needs proper nourishment in order to be able to produce proper designs. Keep lots of water handy. Be sure to take breaks in between designing and make sure to exercise your eyes since you will be looking at a computer screen all day long - designing, completing masterpieces.

Eye Exercises For Graphic Designers Who Stare At Computers

We all know that the skill of graphic design doesn't require hard or intensive physical labor, thankfully. But this skill requires a lot of time and patience in order to improve. It also sure does get wearing when designers can't move from their desk until a project is complete. The computer is and will always be a digital designers work station. As it is, any job can get mentally straining after some time. After plenty of hours, toppled upon hours per week, staring at a digital screen all day can hurt your eyes.

There have been studies and research that have recommended that individuals who are stuck at their computer all day, need to start doing eye exercises to minimize any strain or stress on the eyes. Participating in eye exercises, helps eye muscles become stronger, helps focus and vision, and is good for the eyes. The exercises also stimulate vision at the center of the brain, according to wedmd.com. Some techniques include: moving the eyes side to side, covering one eye and reading with only one, or having one eye follow a repetitious pattern. Widening, closing, and blinking all helps with keeping your eyes healthy.

Graphic designers, when you are staring at your computer screen all day long, make sure to take small regular breaks. Also turn down the screen brightness.

Help Small Business Growth With Graphic Design

Since graphic designers have the ability to either help a small businesses grow or destroy their brand, the pressure is on. The pressure is on to make the company owner satisfied with the end work. Using previous knowledge about composition, lighting, spacial composition, shapes, color, lines, white space, and text, will ensure to give your client a top quality product design.

Don't be afraid to layer. Layering adds detail, intricacy, and depth. Pay attention to efficiency when working on a design.

Layering your work with shapes, lines, colors, distortion tools and filters will only add to the creativity at play, be sure to remember that no one likes looking at a cluttered project full of chaos, or do they?

Placement is everything when it comes to using the digital tools that gratefully exist via sweet technology. When firstly designing a new company graphic, be excited to know that you, the graphic designer,are aiding the economy with small business growth. You are the creator, the artistic visualization and illumination that progresses the company forward. Good looking designs that represent a company with valuable light enable the business to thrive. If your designs follow the companies motto with precise yet creative visualization, then you have done your job and you are on track as a graphic designer.

Visualization

The industry of graphic design needs personalities that exemplify individuals that are the dreamers of society. The visualizers of society. The world of graphic design needs to exist to glue the gap between words and images, the internet and the human eye. People who enjoy seeing and making images must be in this craft and must be able and willing to consistently change. Millions upon millions of individuals search the internet each day looking at images, visualizing, and living precariously through these images.

The internet has opened the doors to a global world that was once closed and never seen. Using graphic design for propaganda is not advised, although freedom of speech is highly regarded. Graphic designers have the ability to distort the minds and views of people. Graphic designers need to use their highly qualified skills to advance society for the betterment of human life. Graphic designers need to use their skill to help and collaborate with others to create a helpful and moving idea. Images will continue to circulate around online and within the i.o.t. (internet of things).

Graphic Design Quotes By Famous People:

So, I'm always around video games but I've always been interested in them from a visual perspective, with the graphic design and that whole thing. I don't know if that comes from my love of photography or what but that's always what's held my interest about them.
-Sophia Bush

If you always put limit on everything you do, physical or anything else. It will spread into your work and into your life. There are no limits. There are only plateaus, and you must not stay there, you must go beyond them – - Bruce Lee

Twenty years from now you will be more disappointed by the things that you didn't do than by the ones you did do. So throw off the bowlines. Sail away from the safe harbor. Catch the trade winds in your sails. Explore. Dream. Discover

– Mark Twain

Failure is built into creativity... the creative act involves this element of 'newness' and 'experimentalism,' then one must expect and accept the possibility of failure.
— Saul Bass

Graphic Design, which fulfills aesthetic needs, complies with the laws of form and exigencies of two-dimensional space; which speaks in semiotics, sans-serifs, and geometrics; which abstracts, transforms, translates, rotates, dilates, repeats, mirrors, groups, and regroups, is not good design if it is irrelevant.

-Paul Rand

If I was influenced by anything, it was architecture: structure having to do with logic. If you don't do it right, the whole thing is going to cave in. In a certain sense, you can carry that to graphic design. Fortunately, however, nobody is

going to die if you do it wrong.
-Paul Rand

I've come up through art school, through painting, through graphic design, through advertising, through TV commercials and music video. I've designed books, built billboards, matchbooks, corporate identities. I continuously paint, I've done conceptual art pictures.
-Tony Kaye

I wear a lot of different hats - from writer to producer and artist. We all do 5 or 6 jobs, everything from creating our own graphic design to actually recording and the whole bit.

-William Bell

When I studied graphic design, I learned a valuable lesson: There's no perfect answer to the puzzle, and creativity is a renewable resource.
-Biz Stone

I always wanted to be a filmmaker and became one through sheer single-mindedness. I came to filmmaking from a background in graphic design. I went to film school at Newcastle Polytechnic.
-Neil Marshall

I got into university to study graphic design, and I got into drama school as well, so I had the choice whether I wanted to go down the sensible route or if I wanted to become an actor.

-Chris Geere

I was always interested in art at school, and after year twelve, senior year, I spent three years studying graphic design at college. I worked in advertising for two years but didn't like it much, then began doing a bit of illustration work for various publishers.
-Graeme Base

I decided to go to school for advertising and graphic design. That was what I was gonna do but acting is that thing, it's like a splinter in your mind and you can't get rid of it. So I decided to move to L.A. a few years ago and it just snowballed into this thing called 'The Hunger Games.' - Dayo Okeniyi

These graphic designers above, show their proper respects to the art of graphic design. The statements above claim that graphic and digital design can be intertwined with all types of different art. This new type of digital art seems to have no boundaries, which is basically what every artist dreams and searches for. Any graphic designer who hones this skill should share their designs, their perceptions, and their visualizations with the world, as it could be the right image to make the perfect change, design history.

Graphic Design End Note

We went over the origination of graphic design. We found out that graphic design didn't really hit the market rampantly until the eighties and nineties. We clearly know the salary of a graphic designer, yet we know that graphic design is not just some type of get rich scheme. Hard and intelligent work is required. Graphic designing is meant for artists. The new-age type of artists. Artists who love technology, software, systems and computers.

The median salary of a graphic designer ranges anywhere from $50,000 - $85,000 USD, depending on experience, education and other factors. We now know that graphic design freelance work provides the working person with more freedom. A freelancer can work wherever they want, as long as the designer has his or her computer and software with them. They do not have to answer to a boss. In addition, the freelance graphic designers are able to set their own hours.

Any individual seeking out graphic design, who doesn't have strong motivation, dedication, perseverance and spine, another career path you shall seek. Graphic designers need to get used to being rejected; proposals are a sales and numbers game. Clients are either found by cold calling, direct contact, direct mailers, email, and/or freelancer sites. If a graphic designer happens to be hungry enough, the graphic designer will then gain momentum and land jobs.

Always be sure to ask for referrals when you finish projects. Make sure to always make the client happy with the final outcome of the design.

When designing a graphic, the artist always needs to ask themselves, 'What am I trying to accomplish?' 'Who is my target audience?'

Make sure to know what your idea and purpose is before creating, as every single company has a unique and different goal.

As stressed throughout the book, always educate yourself on Photoshop, Illustrator, or any design software. Not only will researching Google help, but watching YouTube videos can prove to work as well. The tools are there, there are shapes, text, colors, lighting, filters. Many images or logos can be created or distorted, you are the creator, you decide. There is no limit as to what you can or can't create.

Conclusion

This about rounds up the whole book. Hopefully you have enjoyed reading this book on graphic design and are able to go out and practice what you have just learned.

Remember that graphic design is just like any other skill. The more you learn and practice, the better you become. Continue learning and continue developing your skills.

It is now your time to shine. Practice makes perfect. Apply what you have learned and start designing. Like any other artist, let your dreams fly and let the inspiration flow through you.

Much love,
Jennifer Inston

Printed in Great Britain
by Amazon